Mirror

Bea McKenzie

BookLeaf Publishing

India | USA | UK

Presentation by *BookLeaf Publishing*

Web: www.bookleafpub.com

E-mail: info@bookleafpub.com

ISBN: 9789358317282

First edition 2023

DEDICATION

To the man who held a mirror up to me and
made me love myself, even if he himself could
not love me.

ACKNOWLEDGEMENT

Thank you to my beautiful friends who have held me - literally and figuratively - through my pain.

Energy

When she is strong enough
She will allow herself to feel
The energy in the room again, and
Her world will become a lot smaller
And a lot more beautiful.

Unknown

Coming home to myself.
A description that fits.
Because some journeys
Leave you in the drivers seat
Tearing your hair out
Not knowing where you're going next.
The destination ever changing.
One terrifying, possibly wonderful
Unknown.

Dwindling

You tell me
I don't understand unconditional love
Yet here I stay,
A half life lived
"Fine" but nothing more
A flame dwindling without oxygen
For love of a child.

Home

I always thought that Home was a place
With four walls and a roof.
You made me realise
That home is a feeling in my belly
A space where I'm unapologetically me.
It's vibrating on the same frequency
And speaking without words.
Without these things
Bricks and mortar
Don't mean shit.

Golden

5

Your scent lingers
Woven through my hair,
As you have woven yourself
Slowly but steadily
Through the tapestry of my life.
Golden stitches,
Teasing me with glimmers
Of how my life could look
Were that scent to remain.

Sensation

6

You feel like
Sunsets and sunrises,
Dancing in thunderstorms,
Woodsmoke in the autumn,
Spring sun on my back,
Dewy spiderwebs,
A soft gentle finger down my breastbone,
And kisses planted on my forehead.
Hot sweet tea on cold mornings.
The rush on diving into cold water.
Sensation embodied.

Between the lines

Reading between the lines
Of every message
Love is woven in.
Love
And care
And hope.
Between every trait noticed
Every piss taken
Every tentative "thinking of you".
Because we are
Thinking of each other
With love,
Always.

One foul swoop

Do not let me down gently.
If you're going to let me down
Do it in one foul swoop.
Say the hard words,
And crush all my hope.
Because if even a flicker remains
I will not give up
On a future "us".

90%

9

Right now
My brain is 90%
Making gentle love to you
In a thunderstorm

Nothing, and everything

"What are you thinking?"
You ask
When you catch me staring.
Flashing images,
Of firelight dancing on naked skin
Tender kisses in the rain
Stolen moments in cosy nooks
Tongues on wet flesh
The sweet release it would be
To finally have my wicked way with you.
But I bite my lip, take a deep breath
And say "Nothing, and everything".

Reason

I've spent months
Searching for a reason.
It's occurred to me
That maybe the Universe
Decided it was finally time
I had something to write about.

Firelight on honey

12

I look at the picture you took of me
And realise that you make me glow
Like a golden hour sunset
Or firelight on a jar of honey
Moonlight on water
A candle to a page.
And I get it now.

Room

If I walked into a room
Filled to the brim with everyone I'd ever met,
My legs would carry me to you
Without question.

As-yet unfinished

Tonight it's struck me
How tragic it is
That "us"
Only exists in pages
Of an as-yet unfinished book.

Love and fear

15

Love and fear.
That's what
Everything comes down to.
Fear has been my friend
These past years
But love?
She and I have some
Catching up to do.

A piece of me

Be gentle with that piece of me
You carry with you.
I don't think you know you have it.
But it's in every ray of sunshine warming your
back,
Every sweet scent carried on gentle breeze,
Every crackle of every fire,
Every full moon,
Every warm gulp of tea,
Every dream,
Every smile from every stranger.
So be mindful
Of that piece of me that you carry
For it was not parted with lightly.

Knotted intricately

17

When I said I wanted you
You thought I meant I wanted your body
But the truth is
I want to enter your mind
And make a home there.
I want your soul
To intwine with mine,
Knotted intricately,
Our lives intrinsically woven together.

Hope

And all at once
I had hope
And with hope I had fear.
For when I had no hope
I had nothing to lose.

Rain

Twenty six dates and it's never rained for us
Except for the day you stroked my cheek with
your thumb
And told me
"In another life".
The heavens truly opened that day,
And I like to think that was the Universe
lamenting
The loss of something that could've been
beautiful.

Embers

20

Yesterday I felt like you'd pissed on my fire,
Smothering the inferno burning in my chest.
Today I see there's still a hint of glowing
embers,
And, with time and care
My fire can and will burn again.

In another life

In another life
I'd make us cups of tea in bed
On early foggy mornings
For I know we both like to rise with the sun.
In another life
We'd sit in fields watching the stars
Fingers interwoven, chatting about nothing.
In another life
We'd make love by the crackle of a fire
For I know we both love it's warmth.
In another life
We'd be each other's adventure
And each other's home.
In another life
You might just have let yourself love me.

9 789358 317282